How I B
MUMMY

How I Became a MUMMY

WRITTEN AND ILLUSTRATED BY

LEENA PEKKALAINEN

The American University in Cairo Press

Cairo   New York

Leena Pekkalainen is a writer, blogger, and artist who studied Egyptology at Manchester University. Together with Mr. Mummific, who appeared on her sketchpad one day when she was taking a break from her studies, she writes about ancient Egypt on www.ancientegypt101.com.

First published in 2016 by
The American University in Cairo Press
113 Sharia Kasr el Aini, Cairo, Egypt
420 Fifth Avenue, New York, NY 10018
www.aucpress.com

Exclusive distribution outside Egypt and North America by I.B.Tauris & Co Ltd., 6 Salem Road, London, W4 2BU

Dar el Kutub No. 8051/16
ISBN 978 977 416 811 6

Dar el Kutub Cataloging-in-Publication Data

Pekkalainen, Leena
    How I Became a Mummy / Leena Pekkalainen.—Cairo: The American University in Cairo Press, 2016.
      p.   cm.
      ISBN 978 977 416 811 6
      1. Mummies — Egypt (Ancient) — Study and Teaching

1 2 3 4 5   20 19 18 17 16

Designed by Carolyn Gibson
Printed in China

CONTENTS

About Mummies, Skeletons, and Ash-folks

Now, we all know mummies are wonderful. If anyone disagrees, I would ask: who are the visitor magnets of any museum, hmm? Yes, quite right. Us. The mummies.

Some consider mummies icky (yes, I know, very strange). Now, if our embalmers hadn't done their work properly, we really *would*

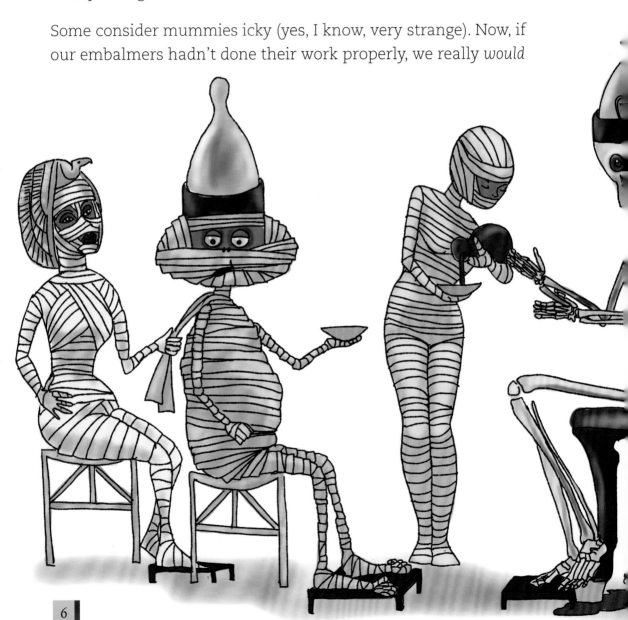

look icky by now—if we existed at all, that is. But as our embalmers knew what they were doing, we are in a much better state, afterlife-wise, than you. Seriously, we have been observing your burial methods with concern. I mean really—if you are not embalmed, all you are left with is a skeleton.

I tell you, the skeleton-folks are not very popular in the afterlife. They are way too thin to please the eye, and it is very hard for them to keep themselves together during outdoor activities. Such a job to gather their missing bones after a little walk in the countryside. . . . Also they are not favored guests at any dinner party. Ever seen a skeleton eat? No, I bet not. A very messy business, and the servants have to clean up afterward. . . . Anything a skeleton chews falls right through them to the seat and the floor. You would not expect them to need food any more, but they still like to eat. A very unfortunate combination, as you do have to be polite and invite them to dinner sometimes. If you spend eternity with someone, you simply can't avoid socializing with them.

The only ones who are happy to have skeletons at dinner are the family dogs. Skeletons never feel full no matter how much they eat, so they eat a lot, with all the dogs gathered around them. The dogs don't have to eat for days after such a visit. You'll have to roll the dogs off into corners of the house after your bony guests have gone home, or you'll trip over them while they are digesting the feast. Some of my dogs have eaten so much that their mummy wrappings burst.

And how about your habit of cremating your dead into ashes? Really, you give no chance to those unfortunates at all. . . . We consider the burning of a body the most horrible thing. Imagine trying to communicate with a heap of ash—do you think that's easy? If someone sneezes, you'll spend days trying to put your dusty old self back together again—if you manage it at all. I have heard stories of dead people who have vanished completely as a result of a windy day. We didn't use the burning of a body to ashes as a method of punishment in our time without reason. . . .

But we, the mummies—we were properly prepared for the afterlife. Our bodies are perfect; much better than in physical life, we believe. Personally I am quite proud of my mummified complexion. Yes, it takes some oiling to keep the skin supple—I think perhaps they used too much salt in my embalming process—but we have excellent cosmetic companies in the afterlife. I prefer the basic oils, but the missus (or my 'Great Royal Wife' as her official title goes) . . . oh my, she can spend fortunes on oils that are meant to lift the wrinkles and give you back a youthful complexion. Ever heard of a non-wrinkly mummy? Neither have I. (And, by the way, I have seen jewelry suspiciously like mine adorning the mummies of the cosmetic companies the missus frequents.) Women are such eternal optimists when it comes to cosmetics. . . .

Anyway, back to the subject at hand. Let me tell you how I acquired my eternal mummy form. It took a little carving, and drying, and wrapping, and such, but the end result is . . .

. . . well, this!

Quite handsome, I'd say, no matter what the missus thinks. She has this unfortunate habit of weaving linen all the time, and when everywhere is filled with linen strips, she finds something to use them on: namely me. A most unpleasant occurrence— she wraps me so tightly I can barely move, and uses so much linen I can hardly walk afterward because my arms and legs are stiff as wands. So I take every opportunity to sneak out to the world of the living, just to keep my comfy old clothing. Also, if I feel she is eyeing my wrappings with that special expression, I invite skeletons to dinner. I can keep my own clothes (I mean wrappings) that much longer when the missus has to rewrap the dogs.

But back to mummification—turn the page and I'll tell you how I became a mummy.

How I Died

And who was I, you ask? I was a pharaoh, and still am. I only use my nickname these days, as there are too many pharaohs in the afterlife for us to take each other seriously. If there is a meeting of the kings, and everyone uses all their formal names, it takes forever and a day to address each other.

Now, of course, we do have forever to state each other's names, but sometimes it's just so boring, everyone greeting everyone else. Sometimes it takes so much time that we forget the reason we even met.

So after a few hundred years of being polite to every king we meet, we usually start calling each other by nicknames. My name turned into Mr. Mummific. You busy people of today's world find even that too long—I have even been called Mr. M. Well, that's all right by me. As long as you keep on saying my name, I remain happy in the afterlife.

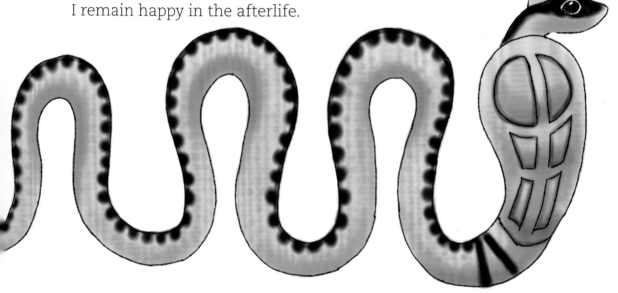

Times were good when I ruled—not too many wars, and riches flowed into my palace. I was pleased with the land, and the land was pleased with me. Peace and prosperity made people wish I would never die (which was my wish, too). I declared myself a living god, as was proper for someone in my position, and though I knew in my heart of hearts that I would die one day, I expected that day to be far in the future. Why wouldn't it? I had good food, was protected by my soldiers, and had interesting discussions with the wisest people of the land. All was well.

There was nothing to threaten me, and a horde of servants took great care of my comfort. They even hid me from the missus if I was too tired to listen to her stories of weaving linen, and who had married whom, and what our chosen heir had been up to. The heir I had chosen unfortunately died before me, so we had to make do with the one son we had left. Later on, when he became king, I heard he created quite a turmoil in the land. But what can you expect from someone who spent his childhood days with his nose in old manuscripts and who didn't take part in any wars? Too much reading and too little physical exercise as a youngster can give you strange ideas about life.

So I enjoyed my life, ate good food, and drank the best wines. I had hundreds of wives to entertain me with song, and dance, and storytelling. My body was handsome and round; this was much respected in the land of Kemet (or, as you now call it, Egypt). Having enough food to gain weight was nowhere near as common as it is in your times. Only the well-to-do could afford to eat that much.

My only trouble was my teeth. I enjoyed honey: honeyed wine, honey cakes, plain old honey. . . . Unfortunately, that had an effect on my chewing tools—that, and the sand that was in everything I ate. Living in a river valley in the midst of a desert had its problems. Sand was literally everywhere: in the food, in the houses, in the clothing, and even in areas of my body that I do not dare mention— you'll have to use your imagination.

Anyway, I woke up one morning, feeling unusually light and pleasant. I rose from the bed and headed for the balcony to watch the sunrise. It was sort of a pharaonic duty to greet the rising sun and show it respect. So there I was, moving along the corridor, wondering why my body felt so light. Usually, walking was rather a

slow business—I had acquired a round form, as I mentioned, and it is slow walking with such a handsome physique. And strangely, my teeth didn't hurt.

Then I began to wonder why no one I met showed any signs of respect toward me. The bodyguards leaned lazily against the wall, the servant girls were gossiping and laughing while I walked past, and my very own vizier just hurried past me on his way to my bedroom, a little late as usual. He often took part in the sun greeting rituals with me.

And then I heard him yell—a yell of surprise. And then everything was chaos. People running, whispering in frightened voices. The missus ran from the women's rooms, looking scared.

"Fetch the heir to the palace! Protect him!" she yelled.

Fetch my heir? Whatever for? Why would my heir need protecting when I was alive?

Well, despite enjoying the good things in life, my mind was still sharp. So the creepy thought hit me almost immediately. I lifted my hands in front of my face . . . and I could see through them! Also there were no rings on my fingers: I always wore lots of rings and other gold jewelry. I loved gold—so much so actually that I would have put your modern Christmas trees to shame.

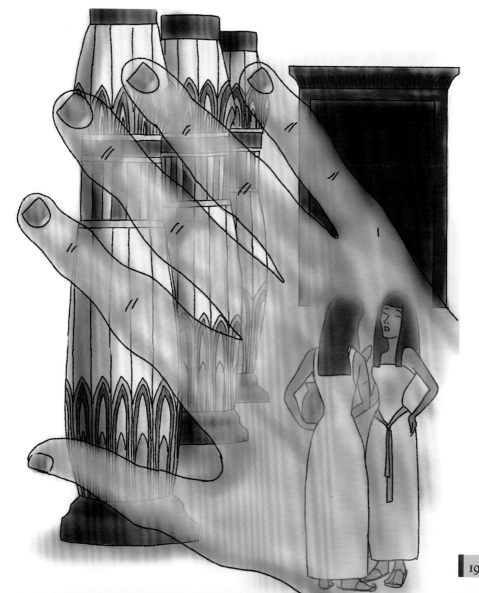

3 Dangling from the Ceiling

While I was staring at my naked self in disbelief, a gust of northerly wind blew through the doors. Usually, we enjoyed the cool breeze, but now to my horror the wind grabbed me and I started floating with it, with no means to stop myself! The doors to my room were ajar, and it must have been sheer luck that the wind pushed me upward and left me floating against the ceiling. A most undignified position, but fortunately it appeared that no one could see their naked king, dangling from the ceiling. That would have been most embarrassing.

I felt some relief; at least I would not fly up into the sky. Still, I very much wanted to return to my body lying below.

I had died in my sleep, it seemed. My body was surrounded by the vizier, the missus, and guards. More guards kept the curious servants and members of the court at a distance. I could see their feet through the doorway from my vantage point.

Then there were more hurried steps, the spectators stepped aside, and a priest came into the room. I knew him well: Meryptah, the high priest of Amun at Ipet-Isut (or Karnak as you know it these days). With him were other priests, who were carrying a stretcher. A few of the servants were now allowed in, and using the bed linen they hoisted my body to the stretcher. The priests staggered somewhat—I had never realized how big I really was, but now, stuck to the ceiling, I had no other option but to take a good look at myself. Maybe a little less honey cake and fine wine might have been a good thing, I had to admit. There seemed to be such a thing as being too 'handsome'. . . .

The high priest opened a roll of papyrus theatrically in front of him and started reading spells.

"You really let yourself go, didn't you?" a faintly familiar voice next to me suddenly said.

I turned my head to find a transparent mummy figure floating in the air next to me.

"I beg your pardon?" I was most offended. "I am the king, and you can't have a king looking like a stick insect—he needs to be round to be respected! And who are you?"

"The king? Not any more," it said. "Not here, at least. You are now a ghost, and a lot needs to be done so that you get your body back." The mummy took my hand and yanked me down from the ceiling to the floor. I was somewhat offended by this, as it was never proper to touch a king without permission, but I have to admit that I was relieved to have my feet on the ground again. Well, sort of. We remained floating a little above the floor. The people in the room totally ignored us— they clearly could not see us at all.

We stood there and watched the high priest finish his reading. Someone bounced into the room through the door: my heir, who had clearly just woken up. The missus immediately moved to his side, and everyone bowed down before the scrawny young man. Or maybe they bowed down before the missus, I'm not quite sure. . . . She was—and is—a formidable personality. You don't want to cross her. But whatever the case, my companion was right. I was no longer an earthly monarch.

"Some king!" my companion snorted, pointing at my heir. "Had I not died, I would have been a *proper* king. I raced chariots, could shoot an arrow and throw a spear. I had muscles!"

He bent his arm to show his biceps. I did not have the heart to tell him that there was not much there to look at, because I now recognized him. He was my elder son, the one who should have been king but had died as a teenager. He sighed, looking at his stick-like arm, clearly aware of his present form. He had always been a sensible person, had never denied the facts of life and death.

"Oh well. I *used* to have muscles. But in any case, I am here to keep an eye on you, so that you stay near your body until it's ready to receive you again. Come on, Dad, let's follow your body to the place of washing."

My body was covered with a sheet of linen, and carried out of the room. The women had begun to wail their grief in the women's quarters.

And so my earthly remains were carried in solemn procession out of the palace, with priests and soldiers in front of and behind the stretcher. The missus and the new king followed after it. We floated right behind them, but of course they could not see us.

And here the mummification began. This isn't for the faint of heart. Be warned: gore galore ahead.

4 Washing

Messengers were sent out across the land to let everyone know I had died. It seemed to me that the court had been expecting my demise, and had the *She-Netjer* tent at the ready. It could not have been more than an hour before my body was taken out of the palace, covered with a large linen cloth—but the tent already stood by the lake, which I had ordered to be dug near the palace (very handy for bringing in supplies for the palace through a canal from the Nile, not to mention all the religious boat trips to temples I was expected to visit in my beautiful ship).

On the other hand, looking at the priests, I think they rather enjoyed the situation and did not hurry the procession in any way. With solemn expressions, they enjoyed the horrified looks of the spectators, and the screams and cries of the ladies of the palace. These women had gathered ashes and were sprinkling them all over themselves, as was the custom, and grieved with loud voices. The pulling of their hair was a bit difficult, though, as many of

them had shaved themselves bald to avoid lice and were wearing wigs—but the ones who had their own hair (like the Great Royal Wife, who refused to cut her beautiful locks) made a great show of it, falling on their knees, raising their hands to the sky, and wailing. Drama queens, to say the least. However, the missus didn't fall to her knees. She walked erect, pushing our heir in front of her, clearly wishing he had a more kingly posture.

What was the *She-Netjer*, or Hall of the Gods, you ask? It was the tent where the bodies of royalty were washed after their death, before the actual mummification process began. The non-royals were washed in a tent as well, only theirs was called the *Ibu*, or Pure Place.

My deceased son never let go of my hand, for which I was grateful, as the wind would probably have carried me to the red lands of the desert. And from there . . . who knows where? He seemed to have control of his ghostly body, whereas I was floating without any means to go where I wanted. But then again, I would not have known where I wanted to go even if I'd had the means. I hadn't been dead before, so how could I have known where it was safe to go?

From our high vantage point, I could see that the great gates of the palace were closed, and my soldiers were standing everywhere on guard. Messengers were running from the palace to announce my death to the good people of Kemet.

While this happened, the procession carrying my earthly remains had reached the washing tent by the lake. And there everyone else had to stop except the priests. The embalming process was a jealously guarded secret of the embalmers. Sons followed in the footsteps of their fathers, so that their secrets would not be revealed to outsiders. And the people of my court were outsiders, and thus were not let in.

We, my son and I, could enter the tent, of course. Much to my surprise, I saw that they had managed to haul a big stone bed in there—they really *must* have been expecting my demise, as there was no way to move such a large stone bed there in an hour. . . .

The bed had raised sides, and they hoisted my body onto the center of it. I was so round that it was rather undignified, especially as my body was quite relaxed at this stage and tried to loll in every conceivable direction.

After a lot of huffing, and puffing, and bad language (in subdued voices so that the retinue standing outside the tent did not hear), I was finally lying on my back on the stone slab. With interest, I noticed that my body's color had begun to change to a definite gray hue. I didn't look very fresh any more, and an inquisitive fly landed on my face. I was most insulted that no one bothered to notice. Instead they were rubbing their backs and mumbling obscenities about my physique. If I had been alive, I would have ordered them to be taken to the stone quarries for such behavior.

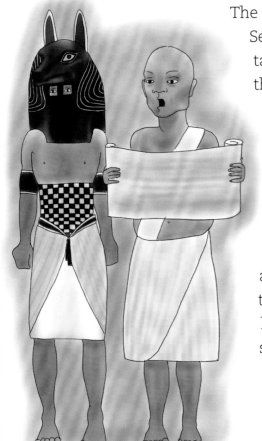

The priest in charge, the Overseer of the Secret, stood at the head of the stone table. He had placed the mask of Anubis, the god of mummification, on his head. Another important priest, the seal-bearer of the god, stood next to him, and a lector priest hurriedly rolled open a papyrus with the appropriate spells. He took a deep breath and began to read with great gusto, in order to assure that my passage to the afterlife began well—and to make sure that the people outside the tent heard him nice and loud. I heard a communal sigh from the throngs outside.

This was when the embalmers started to work with my body. They took off my linen shirt. My son made disapproving noises when he saw my ample form without any coverings.

"Honestly, Dad, that's not a pretty sight. . . . A little more exercise would have been good for you! How many years since your last hunting trip?"

I pretended I was not listening, as it was rather embarrassing to have my own teenage son comment on my naked self. I peeked over the embalmers' shoulders to see what they were about to do.

First, they took a razor and started shaving my face. I understood that—stubble looks so untidy. My servant had shaved me the previous day, but a beard is persistent; it grows no matter what you do. The embalmers used a very beautiful razor for shaving, with jewels in it. It looked much more valuable than my own razor, which I considered inappropriate. Had I known that my priests owned such a valuable razor, I would have demanded it be given to me!

They were quite rough-handed when they stretched my chubby cheeks this way and that to get all the stubble off. If my servant had shaved me like that, I would have sent him to the quarries, along with those foul-mouthed embalmers.

Then the embalmers shaved other parts of my body—which were well shaved, too, but obviously the rituals required giving them renewed attention. They raised my arms to reach my armpits, and then made sure my limbs were smooth as a baby's bottom—not that I know much about the skin of babies; they were taken care of by the women, and I only became interested in them when they could talk. Communication is so much easier when both parties use words instead of shrieks and ga-gas.

When they began to shave my intimate parts, I made it my business to float in front of my son in a vain attempt to block his view—which was pretty desperate, considering that he could see through me. It has to be said that to his credit he pretended to be looking in a different direction altogether.

Next, two embalmers took jugs filled with liquid and lifted them above my body. The lector priest continued reading spells, and the men began to pour the liquid over me. Just a moment . . . it was palm wine! I almost felt that this was a gross misuse of the beverage, but then I realized that preparing my royal body for the afterlife required the very best of materials. If I was to be bathed in wine, so be it. The gods know, it was no stranger than all the things the women of the palace used on their skins to stay youthful.

My skin was wiped with linen cloths—these were new and most likely woven by my missus and her ladies. They ran a veritable linen business from the palaces; there was a neverending market for shrouds in our culture, as every mummy had to be wrapped in linen.

The raised sides of the table kept the liquid on top of it, so it was easy for the men to dip their cloths into the wine and continue washing. Once they considered their job well done, they pulled out a plug from a drain at the corner. As the surface of the table sloped, the wine trickled out into a waiting jar. This was not thrown away. (No, they didn't drink it! It was to be buried later).

After this, it was time to wash my body with another kind of liquid, namely water from the Nile. New spells were recited, this time mentioning how I was crossing the lake safely to be transfigured into an ancestral spirit—very fine words of which I understood very little.

"What lake are they talking about?" I asked my son.

"The puddle you are lying in, I think," he shrugged. "I've watched quite a few embalmings, and frankly I don't have much idea what those spells are about. I'm not altogether convinced that the priests know, either. But they have always *been* recited, and so they will always *be* recited."

I was a bit surprised at that. After all, in life he had been named as a high-ranking priest to a very large temple. But what can you expect from teenage boys? They are more interested in pretty girls and horses than in religious studies—which is as it should be, I suppose. My living heir being an exception to this rule, as I mentioned. . . .

While I was pondering all this, the embalmers had finished the washing and had let the water run out. Then, to my surprise, they began to hoist me from the stone slab again. This time, the job seemed even more difficult, as I was all slippery.

"What now?" I asked my son. "Is that it? They just wash me?"

"Oh no, now the real fun begins!" He smiled and rubbed his hands together in a way that made me somewhat uneasy. "But they won't gut you here, right next to the palace, because the process doesn't exactly smell sweet. . . . You need to be taken elsewhere for the cutting, and drying, and wrapping parts."

I was placed on a new stretcher, much sturdier than the one I had been carried in on. It had poles at the corners and a canopy stretched over the top. A wooden coffin was placed on it, and they tried to lift me into it . . . but let's just say that my form was too 'overflowing' to fit in there. I am quite sure that I heard one of the men mumble something about a fat hippo, but no one seemed to pay any attention to the insult. Probably because they were busy trying not to pull a muscle.

Eventually, they had to place two wooden boards on the stretcher, and then put my body, lying on its back, on top of them. This way, I did not hang down over the sides of the stretcher in an undignified manner. Then they covered me with a thick cloth and another blanket, beautifully woven in red and green.

The embalmers had a whispered discussion about the matter of carrying my body to the next place. After complaining about the back pains that had resulted from lifting me in the tent, they decided that strong servants were to be called to do the carrying.

They arrived—giving fearful looks at the priests, who posed to full effect, with their Anubis masks, and fine clothing, and religious scrolls—and grabbed the poles of the stretcher.

My son let out an amused giggle at the expressions of the servants when they realized how heavy I was. They tottered for a few moments, trying to balance, and I feared I would slip to the ground from beneath the coverings. Finally, they got my body balanced, the doorway to the tent was opened, and my body continued its journey to the the *Per-Nefer*, the Good House, where sharp knives and tools were already waiting for my arrival.

5 Gutting

"And now for the interesting part," my son announced with an expectant grin, when the stretcher was carried outside to a waiting sled pulled by oxen. Even more priests had arrived, and they formed a long procession before and after the sled.

It took a long while to reach the mud-brick building that had been erected near my tomb in the Valley of the Kings (and an excellent tomb it was, if I may say so—because of my advanced age, there had been plenty of time to put the finishing touches to it). All the way, priests poured milk from jars into the dust to make the sled glide easily.

What? Why use a sled instead of a cart? Well, divinities traveled on sleds, everyone knows that! And I was proclaimed divine during my lifetime, so a sled it was for me.

"What did you mean by 'interesting part'?" I asked my son.

We floated inside the building and could barely fit in—it was already crowded from floor to ceiling. Every place was full of transparent mummified figures using their elbows with great gusto to clear a good observing point for themselves.

I looked at them with my mouth open in astonishment. They waved cheerily at me, clutching their bowls full of munchies, and eventually settled in neat rows all around the embalming table.

"Mummification is great entertainment," my son enlightened me. "And the mummification of a king—well, you have to pay a lot to be able to get a seat."

I was not especially happy with all the crowds observing my naked self on the mummification table.

My son, however, thought nothing of it, and got us a front row seat. I observed the wooden embalming table where I lay. The table in question was slightly slanted and there were raised cross-pieces that kept my body off the actual surface.

"What are those for? The cross-pieces, I mean. Looks uncomfortable." I said to my son.

"That's to help all the fluids to drain. Although, I don't know who would care if a dead body felt comfortable."

That sounded rather messy, and for a while I felt like leaving. Still, I had no option but to stay or be blown away by the desert winds. And the desert was to be avoided at all costs—all our people feared it.

One of the priests remained with the embalmers and kept on reading spells from a scroll. If I hadn't been dead, I am sure I would have fallen asleep listening to his monotone voice.

The embalmers arranged jars, and pots, and sacks, and knives, and hooks around my body (which was definitely a whiter shade of pale by now), checking that they had everything they needed. Then, to my surprise, they all went out and after a while came back with hands full of small rocks. With them was a man who had no rocks, and he looked very sour. The others chuckled expectantly. I didn't understand why.

"Ah, they're not starting with the brain this time. . . ." my son observed.

There was excited movement among the spectators, and a few yips and whoops. Everyone leaned forward when the sour-looking man bent down (the table was rather low) and pulled out a knife with a black obsidian blade. Obsidian is the sharpest thing there is.

Oh great, so now they were going to start gutting me! I wondered why the man didn't squat down by the low table—surely bending down from straight legs was murder to the back. . . .

I got my answer soon enough. He made an incision in the left side of my belly, toward my groin. And immediately the other embalmers started throwing their sharp rocks at him and yelling obscenities about insulting my body. The cutter threw the knife to the floor, ran out of the

mud-brick building, and disappeared.
This charade was apparently all part of the ritual.

But I stared in horror, while the mummified spectators cheered.

"He just cut me!" I said, pointing at the gash on my side, not quite believing what I'd seen, even though of course I knew that this was done to all mummies-to-be.

My son pointed out the obvious. "Well, they can't take out your inner organs without cutting you, can they?"

I could barely hear him—the mummies around us were yelling at each other, passing little amulets forward to one specific mummy who sat cross-legged in the middle of them all. He put the amulets into a small basket next to him and wrote something down on a piece of papyrus.

"What are they doing?"

"Hmm? Oh, they're betting on your intestines, about their length. Great fun, just look!"

I turned my attention back to my body and noticed that someone had squatted on the floor next to it. With a slightly bored look on his face, the man matter-of-factly put his hand into the cut on my skin, negotiated his way through a lot of fat (I will not repeat his comments here, as they were most disrespectful), and started yanking things out so that my round belly bounced up, and down, and sideways.

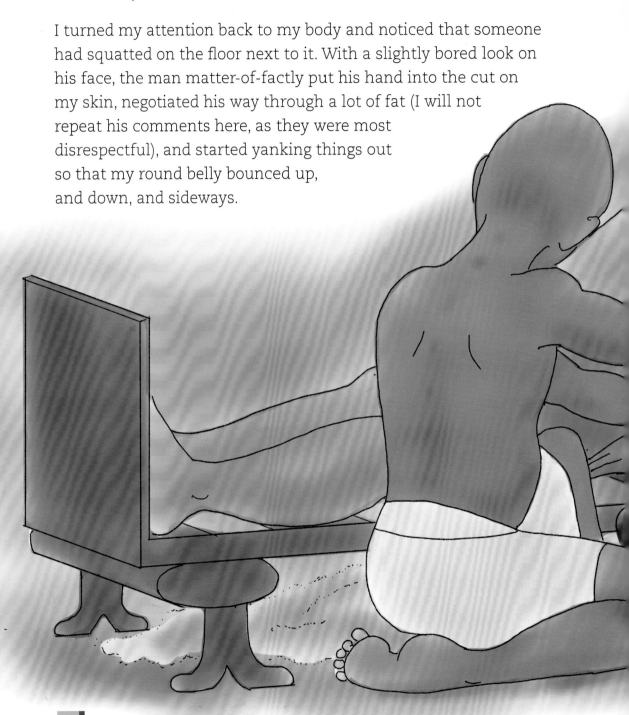

Have you ever seen what's inside your stomach?
No? Well, I don't recommend it. If anyone ever tells you that you haven't got guts, I assure you that you do. Boy, do you have guts!

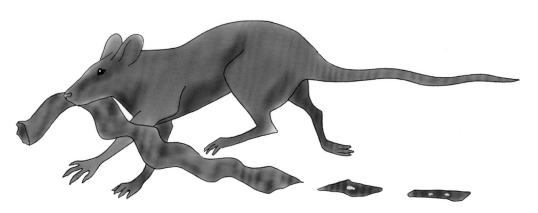

Mine slid out of the cut on my side into a large bowl on the floor. The small intestines were a grayish purple color, and the thicker large intestines were a dark reddish color, and there was blood all over the place. Not a pretty sight! The clean sand beneath the bed absorbed the liquids and was quickly scooped away once my belly had been emptied.

The guts were quickly taken away and washed in the corner of the hut. By the looks on the faces of the embalmers, the scent was not exactly delightful. I did not take a closer look. The priest reading the scroll aloud positioned himself nearer to the doorway, which, though closed with a curtain, let some air in.

One of the mummy ghosts stood right next to the embalmer who was washing my guts. The mummy had a measuring rod and quickly measured my bowels as they slid through the embalmer's hands and into a big jar of water. The embalmer paid no attention to the mumbling mummy, although he shivered when the ghost touched him during the process.

"I remind you all that because we are embalming a pharaoh, we shall use royal cubits as our measurement," the bookie mummy declared aloud.

The spectators agreed that this was the proper procedure.

"And what is the result?" the bookie asked, when all my intestines had been washed. I tried to look the other way.

"Fourteen royal cubits and two palms," was the answer (and for those of you who do not know about ancient Egyptian measurements, that is about seven-and-a-half meters, or twenty-four feet).

Disappointed mumbling came from some of the mummies.

"Surely he should have had more guts, being so fat!" a thin little mummy complained, looking at me accusingly. He looked a lot like one my servants who had died a few years earlier—one who had complained about how carrying all that food to me would break his back. . . .

He had obviously wagered on a longer gut, and sat sourly with his arms crossed while others collected their winnings. His lower lip was hanging so low, I was afraid it would fall off.

In quick succession, another embalmer removed my liver, and stomach, and lungs. There was some betting about whether my heart would be removed inadvertently, but most mummies seemed to believe that the embalmers would be careful and not yank it out. They were correct.

After washing everything that they had dug out of me, they put it into bowls on a side table.

"And now . . . the brains!" My son leaned back and assumed a comfortable position.

6 The Brains

My attention turned to a small group of mummified ghosts who were arguing with each other. One of them held a papyrus scroll up in front of him and tried to read it. He was having some problems, and I understood why when I saw he had no eyes, only two onions that had been stuck where his eyes had been.

The other mummies waved their hands so that linen wrapping fluttered in the air, and I do believe I saw a finger fly off and into the audience, which was enjoying the argument. Someone picked the finger up from the floor and handed it back to the mummy in question. He stuck it between his wrappings and continued arguing.

"What are they doing?" I asked my son.

"Hmm?" He was concentrating on a young female mummy, who wore royal adornments. Not anyone I recognized, so probably not one of my wives.

"Those mummies—what's the problem?"

One of the mummies was so angry that he jabbed a papyrus scroll into one of the spectator's chests. He fell on his back with a loud thump, creating a cloud of dust. Other spectators duly helped the fallen one back to his feet.

"They are the chief embalmers who developed the art of mummification through the ages. They take great interest in the work of the living embalmers, and make surprise inspections to see that the proper procedures are followed," my son informed me.

I wondered what such inspections would achieve, as the living embalmers could not communicate with the dead ones, but my son answered that before I could ask.

"Those embalmers who do their work poorly will be taken to a council of embalmers when they come to the afterlife, and will be punished according to their misdeeds."

"Really?"

"And right now they are arguing whether it is all right not to start the whole process by digging the brains out first," my son clarified. "And whether these embalmers should be reprimanded for not starting with the head."

"Oh, they usually take the brains out first?"

"Yes, most of the time. But it seems they are coming to the conclusion that the embalmers wanted your guts out first because you are so fat, and probably have lots of food in your intestines that would start to rot in no time. Not a pleasant procedure, handling a body that has begun to rot."

I wasn't sure I wanted to talk about this, but luckily the embalmers started the brain-process right then, so I could concentrate on other things.

One of the embalmers took a metal hook that was slightly curved at one end. He placed it inside my left nostril, and then with a brisk movement shoved it in. I heard bone crack.

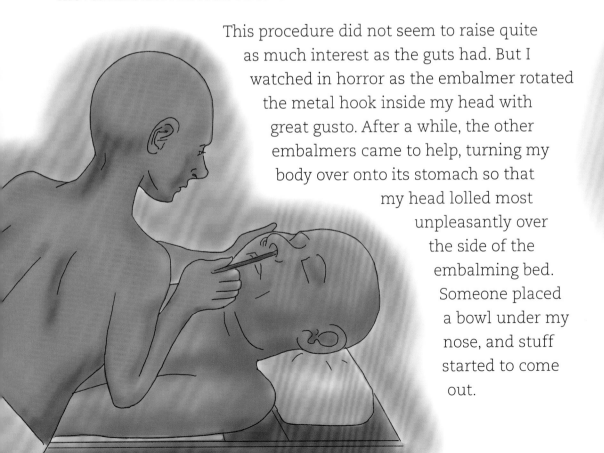

This procedure did not seem to raise quite as much interest as the guts had. But I watched in horror as the embalmer rotated the metal hook inside my head with great gusto. After a while, the other embalmers came to help, turning my body over onto its stomach so that my head lolled most unpleasantly over the side of the embalming bed. Someone placed a bowl under my nose, and stuff started to come out.

At this point, I must say that I do not understand why modern people appreciate the brain. Seriously, just have a look at it in the bowl—it looks like something that came out of a nose! (Oh wait, it *did* come out of a nose!)

All Egyptians know that the brain is nothing but a source of snot. Why the gods chose to create people so that they would have their heads full of snot, I can't say. But the brain clearly has nothing to do with intelligence or thought, as you modern folks think. Oh no, the heart is the center of consciousness and thinking, and you should teach this at your schools (is it true that you have brain surgeons? If so, why?).

Oh well, back to the business at hand.

The men turned my body on its back once again. Someone took a stick, and wrapped linen around it, and stuck this up my nose. More rotating ensued, and when the stick was pulled out, I could see that more snot had stuck to it. After this, another stick with linen around it was shoved inside my head, and another, and another, and this continued until my head was empty.

I seriously think it would have been great if this could have been done to me while I was alive. Just remembering all those colds I had—sneezing was not fun, and if my head had been emptied of snot earlier, life would have been so much easier. . . .

After removing the snot from my head, the embalmers took a jug of palm wine and poured this through the slit on my side, into my body. They drained this out, and then poured water into the cavity. They then added more sand under the embalming bed, and turned my body on its side to let the liquid out, which was no mean feat considering my size. Whatever was left, they soaked up using linen rags.

"Right, now everything is ready for the next phase!" My son clapped his hands, clearly enjoying the show. As a result of him letting go of me, I started to float toward the ceiling, still having no control over my movements. "Oh, sorry." He reached up and caught me as I was drifting helplessly over my body, and yanked me down again.

I felt slightly nauseous after seeing all this mutilation done to my body. (This was interesting in itself, I mean, how can you feel nauseous outside your body?)

"What's that?" My curiosity overcame me.

"Well, now you have been gutted, next you will be salted."

Great. . . .

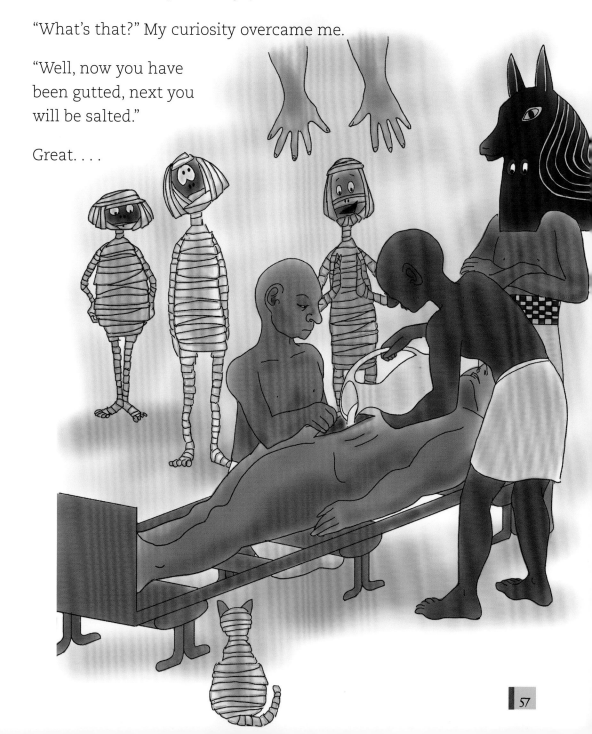

7 Salting

One of the embalmers entered, carrying a beaker filled with something hot; he had wrapped cloth around it so as not to burn his fingers. I soon found out what the stuff was when my body's head was tilted backward and they carefully poured melted resin into my left nostril. Then they unceremoniously pushed linen plugs into my nostrils to stop the resin from coming out again. After this, they rolled resin into two balls and pushed them into my ears. And then . . . they actually put a linen plug steeped in resin into my butt! Now, that was not a very dignified sight—they struggled to find the necessary opening between my rather well formed cheeks, and the whole procedure

caused some chuckling and rather impolite comments in the mummified audience. I made a mental note to haunt my living heir and tell him that he should take physical exercise more seriously.

I noticed some embalmers working on my removed lungs, stomach, intestines, and liver. They washed them with wine and water, and added spices (for a brief moment, the thought came to mind that they were about to start cooking dinner), and then put them on top of a pile of salt on a side table. They poured more salt over them until they were completely covered.

"Why do they do that?" I asked my son, who seemed to be flirting with the young female mummy. That's my boy! He would have gathered a considerable harem had he lived, I am sure. I compared him to my living son, who spent most of his time reading old religious scrolls, and I hoped that the beautiful wife we had chosen for him would manage to lift his nose out of those manuscripts.

"The salt dries them," my son answered over his shoulder, without turning his head from the pretty mummy, who was twirling a piece of linen wrapping over her ear in her fingers, pretending not to notice my son's gaze.

"Aha. . . ."

The embalmers then opened large sacks of salt standing by the wall, and started throwing salt under my body. As the body was lying on top of the raised cross-pieces, they managed to pack the table underneath me with salt as well. They then wiped the body once more with spiced wine, using linen rags.

A younger embalmer, clearly an apprentice, had been squatting by the wall (under a row of mummies, but not paying any attention

to them), making small linen pouches of salt, and now he brought these to his father. The father took the pouches one by one and put them inside my body through the slit on the side.

Then they started pouring salt all over me. The priest, who was almost croaking now after reading from the scroll for so long, raised his voice in new enthusiasm. I am sure I heard a crow reply to him from behind the curtain across the doorway.

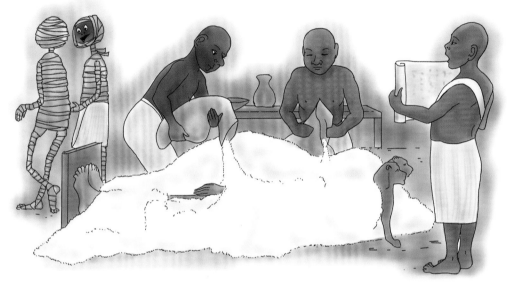

The embalmers covered me completely with salt—which turned out to be quite a task, considering my size, but by using some extra planks attached to the sides of the table they finally managed to make me disappear from sight. The mummified audience seemed to think there was nothing left to see, and they left, counting their winnings from the betting. Only my son and I were left floating there. Most of the embalmers left as well, and only two remained. The lector priest finally stopped reciting, and the sudden quiet made my ears ring (which was odd, considering the physical ears in questions were covered in salt and plugged with resin).

"And now what?" I inquired of my son.

"Now we wait for forty days," he said, clearly a bit grumpy at having to hold on to his dad for so long. The pretty maiden had left, too.

"Forty days? Seriously? But that's boring! Are we supposed to just stand—I mean, float—here for forty days?"

"Hmm. . . ." My son tapped his chin with the forefinger of his free hand. "We don't necessarily need to stay here. We could go and have some fun!"

"Really?" This lifted my spirits considerably. "What can we do?"

"Let's go and ghost around a bit! Nothing cheers a dead person up more than giving a good scare to unpleasant people."

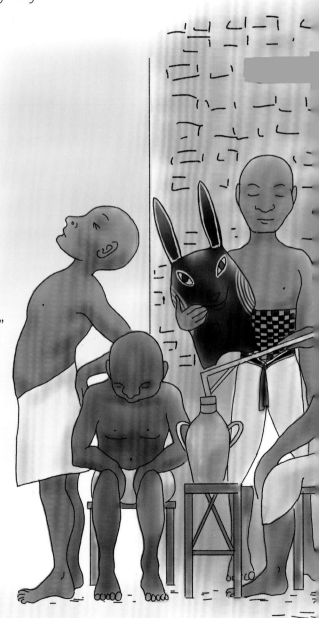

My son unwrapped a long strip of his linen wrappings and tied it around my wrist. As the other end of the wrappings was still attached to him, I bobbed in the air by his side. I considered voicing my objection to 'ghosting around,' but maybe it could be fun. . . . During the last part of my physical life, I had not had much fun, thanks to the constant toothache and being overweight. I hadn't felt this good in years!

"Yes, let's do it!" I said to my son, and he floated us out of the door and past the lector priest, who was now sitting on a little chair, drinking beer with the two remaining embalmers.

8 Ghosting Around

Forty days. During that time, there was nothing much to do but kill time. The embalmers changed the salt every once in a while when it got wet—the salt drew out all my bodily fluids, which of course was the whole purpose of salting my royal self.

The used salt was carefully gathered, just like the wine that had been used to wash me. It was not thrown away, but placed in jars, which would be buried later. It was considered sacred once it had been used in embalming.

My son and I occasionally came back to watch the salting process continue, and it was interesting to see how my plump body slowly shriveled. Quite an effective alternative to dieting, I'd say. (Dieting is something I never understood: If you can eat all you want, why would you not do that?)

"Maybe if I had bathed in salty water, I might not have been so . . . erm, handsome," I wondered out loud.

"Hippo-like, you mean?" My son was no sweet-talker. "You should hope that they manage to shrink you to a decent size, or you won't fit into your sarcophagus and you'll be nicknamed 'Hippo' in the afterlife."

I was mute with shock. That they would call *me*, the greatest king the world has ever seen, a *hippo*? Perhaps if there had been a hippo god, this would be okay, but as far as I could remember there was only a pregnant hippo goddess, Taweret. . . . Maybe I should have paid more attention to the high priest of Amun on his visits, but I suppose I was too busy declaring myself a living god to pay attention to hippo deities.

Still, despite the shock of not being the center of the world any more, I have to admit that I had a lot of fun with my son. We went 'ghosting around,' as he put it.

There is something quite satisfying in scaring people you never liked. Yes, yes, I know it's not good behavior, but what can you expect from someone newly dead? Surely you take what fun you can from the situation. If anyone asks, I'll just say that I wasn't aware of the rules of conduct for the dead yet (just wait and see when it's your turn—I bet you won't act all that dignified yourself).

But anyway, while the embalmers played the game of *senet* next to my drying corpse, and the priest occasionally read a spell or two when he wasn't drinking beer, my son and I visited the people I had known in my life. The servant who always ate some of my food on its way from the kitchen made a rather interesting run for safety when I whispered in his ear that I knew he had been stealing. Rather a surprising reaction, really, as I did not expect him to hear me.

"Some people are more aware of ghosts than others," my son explained. "But I wouldn't have scared him, if I were you."

"Why not?"

"He was only doing his job: testing your food for poison. Mom ordered him to do that, though you probably didn't know it."

"Oh." I felt embarrassed.

The vizier, on the other hand, paid no attention to me. He just sat there, with his droopy cheeks and gloomy expression, listening to messengers from different parts of the country.

I kind of understood his expression. The new king was a teenager and certainly not experienced enough to rule the land.

My Great Royal Wife, however, was more than capable of the task. She sat next to the vizier, and stopped the new king from sneaking out of the room with one look—or several looks, really, as the heir apparent had little enthusiasm for being a ruler and showed a constant tendency to glide toward the door.

"No, you listen to me, or you will never be a great king! Of course your vizier will do everything for you if necessary, but a truly great king knows how to rule his land! You will never gain the respect of the elite if you let others rule for you. So you get your lazy butt here this instant, and sit down, and listen to what the messengers from around Kemet have come to tell us, and how we reply to them," the missus ordered, and the sulky new king had no other choice but to obey.

From my new vantage point, I pitied the boy a little. My Great Royal Wife could be a pain in the . . . royal butt, if you will. I sometimes thought she was the wisest of us when it came to ruling the land—she had practically ruled it for the last few years while I was huffing and puffing and complaining about my toothaches.

So they were all too busy to pay any attention to us, which was just as well—it suddenly dawned on me that if anyone could see me, I still was quite naked, as I had not been wrapped in my bandages yet (my son had assured me that I would no longer be naked once all the proper burial rituals had been performed).

And so, from then on until the end of the forty days of salting, I demanded that we ghost around only after sunset. This was even more effective, as when people are half-asleep they are in a state where it is more likely they will sense ghosts.

We caused a few good scares, one of the most satisfying ones being scaring the bejeebies out of the high priest of Amun just as he went to bed after the evening rituals at the Ipet-Sun, the most sacred of places, the Sanctuary of Amun. Such a pompous person, who seemed to think he ranked higher in the eyes of the gods than I did. . . . I had been told that he had said the temple was richer than the king's court!

It was fascinating how he reacted to my son lifting an oil lamp in the air and moving it around the room.

"You can do that? Can I do it, too?" I clapped my hands together.

"It takes a lot of muscle, so I would say you could not," my son said bluntly. "Physical objects weigh a lot more to us when we are dead than when we were alive."

I observed with interest that the high priest was trying to hide under his blanket in a corner.

"You think he can hear me?"

"Well, you won't know until you try, will you?"

My son dragged me over to the high priest, and I tried to put on a booming voice.

"You shall let the new king rule in peace! You will not meddle in the affairs of state, or else. . . ."

I think he heard me, because he wrapped the blanket even tighter around himself.

"Or else? Can't you come up with something more colorful?" my son snorted.

I thought for a while, but could not think of anything teenage enough.

"I could use a little help here. . . ."

Shortly after, when I had finished repeating the colorful curses my son had whispered into my ear, I was quite happy with the result. The high priest would not peek out from under his shivering heap of blankets until sunrise, I was certain of it.

"And where did you learn such foul language?" I demanded to know.

My son just shrugged and took me out of the high priest's house. We glided over the temple, which was illuminated by the full moon. A beautiful sight.

And when the sun began to color the horizon from black to blue, and then to red, my son said:

"Right, that is the fortieth sunrise since they covered you in salt. Now they'll begin to wrap you. We'd better get back so we can get a good view. The others will begin to appear soon."

At that, we began our journey over the river to the west, where my place of embalming was.

Wrapping

Do you know what a body looks like when it has been dried inside a pile of salt? Like a huge raisin. At least, that's what I looked like, even though the embalmers had tried their best. I mean, I did have a lot of skin around my ample form, but as my muscles and the overall handsomeness had shrunk (I refused to listen to any hippo remarks from my son at this point), all that skin would have made me look like a leather sack. So the embalmers had, at some point, put resin-soaked linen under the skin of my arms, legs, and neck to plump me up a bit, so I had some believable roundness left. I *had* been a man of substance after all. . . .

"Hope they didn't overdo it with the packing," my son said. "If they do, your skin can burst. But you have so much skin. . . ."

To my surprise, the spectators started appearing again, though I thought there was nothing to see. One by one, the mummies appeared around the embalming table and started making bets again. The same scribe mummy as last time sat on the floor, cross-legged, accepted their amulets, and wrote down their wagers. I wondered how he could cross his legs so well—to me, all the mummies seemed to be stiff figures. I asked my son.

"Oh, him. Yes, once he reached the afterlife, he began to exercise a lot. He met a merchant from across the Great Green who came from a country where they spend a lot of time stretching their bodies into strange positions. With time, he became flexible enough to sit down and cross his legs like a proper scribe should. But it did take a lot of effort—and sometimes he got stuck in something like a reef knot, and it took a lot of work to untangle him."

The Great Green? That would be the sea.

Later on, I learned that the exercise ritual resembled the yoga practice of your times—a very strange-looking practice for sure, and certainly not dignified for a king.

"What are they betting on *now?*" I asked my son, slightly annoyed at all the attention the spectators were giving to my body, especially as it now looked less than presentable.

"It is time to bet on how many of your amulets and pieces of jewelry will be stolen at this stage. Obviously most, if not all, of them will disappear in the years to come, but it's interesting to see how many will actually make it to the tomb," my son elaborated.

"Excuse me?! What do you mean, the amulets will disappear in the future?"

My son looked at me like I was a halfwit.

"Well, what do you think? Your tomb will most likely be robbed. There are so many people building it, and so many people carrying all those valuables into the tomb, that some of them are bound to come back to loot the tomb. After all, they know where it's situated, and the guards often happily look the other way if promised a good enough share of the spoils. And now I'll tell you one of the secrets the living have no idea about," my son whispered, as if the embalmers could hear him. "Because we know that the tombs will be looted, we loot them ourselves soon after the burial."

"You *what?*"

"Makes sense, doesn't it? The amulets are meant for you, after all. They are wrapped into your shrouds. When the looters come, they will tear the shrouds away."

"Really? How disrespectful!" I stole a worried look at my raisin-like body on the embalming table. I would not want any living person to see how it looked now, and any robber would undoubtedly do so if they tore my wrappings off. . . .

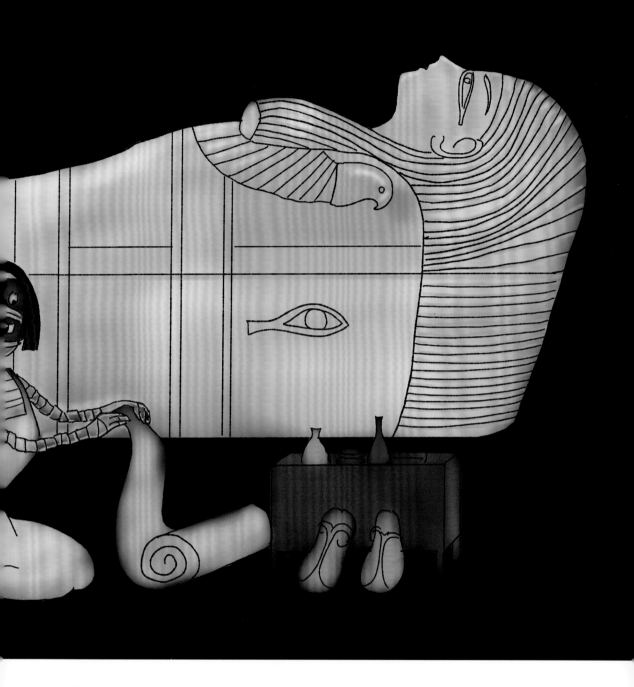

"It is indeed. So once you have become a real mummy, take my advice and collect all the valuables from your tomb that you possibly can. If you wish to live according to your status and have some valuables for trading, you'll need them."

"Trading? There's trading in the afterlife?"

"Yes, but you'll learn all of this later on. Just heed my advice: take whatever you can when you step from your tomb to the afterlife.

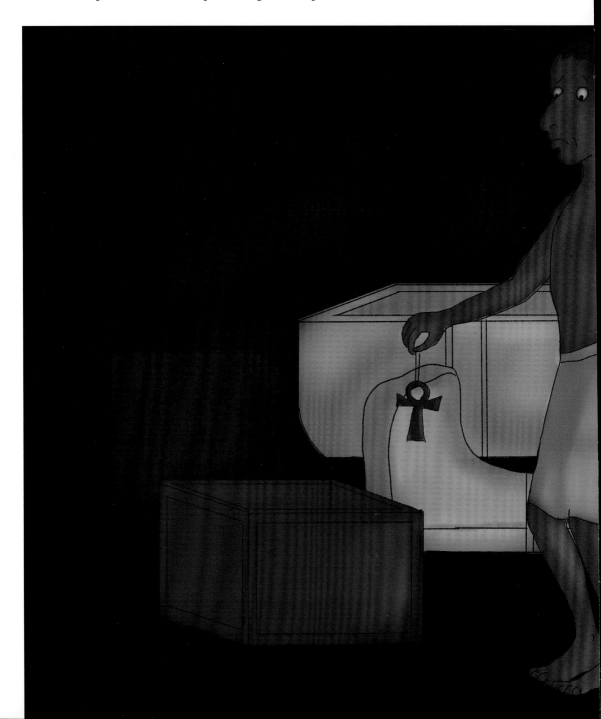

And be prepared to pay other mummies—they will help you carry even more. This way, when the robbers come, and find no mummy and most of the valuables gone, they just think someone beat them to it.

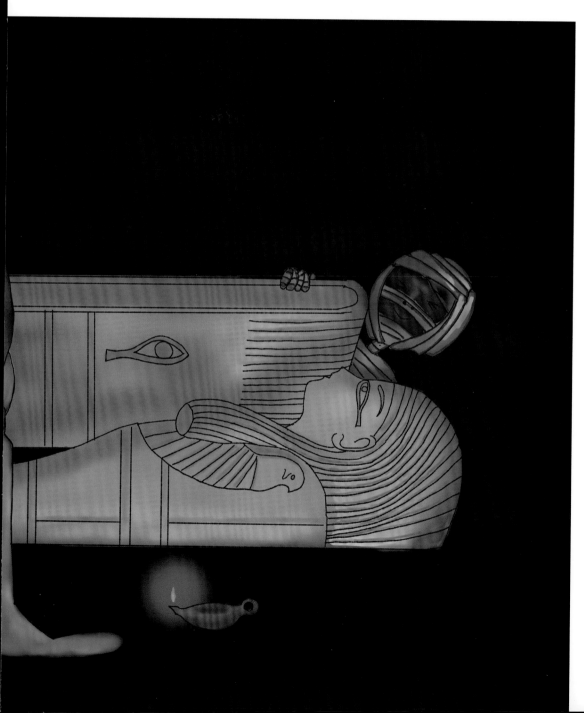

Now, this was something to chew on. Everyone knew of the tomb robbers, of course, but I had never thought that mummies robbed their own tombs!

My son interrupted my musings, and pointed at the embalmers. "Okay, it's time for the oiling."

To my surprise, they did not just start wrapping the linen strips around me. First, they took water from the Nile and washed all the excess salt off my skin. Then they poured expensive, sweet-smelling oils—juniper and cedar, and some others too—onto my skin and rubbed them in. And, believe it or not, the process lasted for days. Oiling, then drying the skin, oiling and drying it again. The mummies came and went, checking out when the oiling would be complete and the wrapping would begin.

"Can't they just get on with it?" I was impatient.

"If they wrapped you while the oils were still wet, you might combust in your coffin," my son told me.

"As in . . . I would burn?"

"Yes, some of those oils begin to burn on their own if not allowed to dry. You'd be turned to charcoal."

Suddenly I was no longer in any hurry.

Finally the embalmers had used all the oils. Carefully they lifted my arms and tried to flex them. Word spread quickly, and all the mummies reappeared. A few mummies bent forward with an expectant look in their eyes—I did not want to know if there were any bets on my arms being snapped off.

But even though my salted body had looked very dry, after all that oiling the arms did flex a bit. The embalmers managed to cross my arms over my chest, which was the proper position for a king. They seemed content with the result.

They started the wrapping by placing two rolls of linen under my body, from the shoulders toward the legs. Now that I'd lost some weight, they seemed to have no problem in lifting my stiff body to manage this.

Then they continued with my head. When they lifted the roll of linen, I realized that it had probably been woven by my missus and her attendants, as the necessary linen strips were provided by the dead person's family. Suddenly I appreciated all the trouble that the women of the royal household took in making linen for the dead. They made it possible for us to be buried decently clothed.

"And the first amulet. . . ." my son observed.

All the mummies bent forward to see better, so there was a real commotion for a while. A few mummies were squeezed so hard that they popped out of the crowd and into the air, fluttering in various directions like dry leaves. Someone collected a loose arm, and one of the mummies seemed to have trouble keeping his head on his shoulders. A friend of his unceremoniously hit him on top of his head to attach it back to his body.

A priest extended a hand, and on it was a small amulet of reddish stone, a tiny headrest amulet. The priest declared to it that its job was to raise my head at resurrection.

Much to the disappointment of the spectators, the amulet was placed under my head and strips of linen were rolled over it, and around my head and neck.

The embalmers stopped there for a while, and turned their attention to my hands and feet. The priest opened a small chest he was holding and I caught a glimpse of gold. The eldest of the embalmers took the chest and removed ten little tubes made of gold. These he carefully placed on my stiff fingers and toes. On a closer look, I realized that they had tied strings around my finger- and toenails, which they had hennaed to a pretty red color— really quite fashionable.

"To protect them so they won't drop off," my son informed me before I had a chance to ask about the strings.

Now the priest turned and opened a bigger chest that had been placed on the floor. Out came a pair of golden sandals—and I mean real gold. The eldest embalmer carefully placed these on my feet. I noticed carvings on the soles of the shoes, and bending closer I saw images of Kemet's enemies, also called the Nine Bows. I nodded. Yes, when I walked with those shoes, I would be trampling on my enemies with every step I took.

One embalmer carefully wrapped my fingers and hands so that the gold finger protectors disappeared from sight. Another concentrated on my feet and did the same.

Two mummies stood right next to them with their noses almost touching the embalmers' hands. When the embalmers started wrapping the arms and legs with overlapping spirals of linen, the mummies straightened themselves with looks of disappointment.

"Nothing stolen there. . . ." my son explained.

A golden plaque appeared; it was placed on the incision they had made to get my guts out, and was decorated with the Eye of Horus.

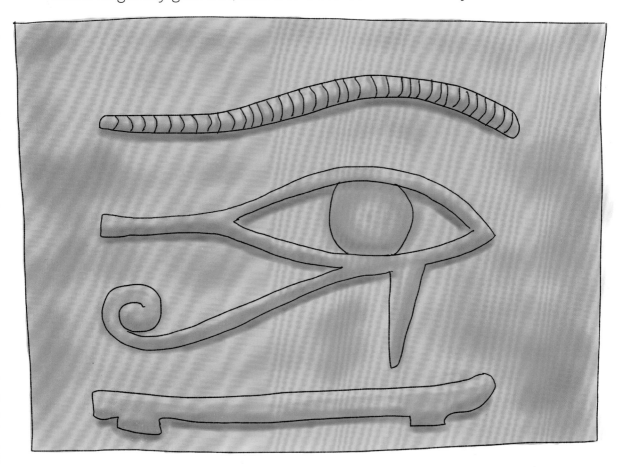

The linen was soaked in good-smelling oils, and before they wrapped it around me they brushed the layer underneath with resin. Once the head, hands, and feet were securely wrapped, they carefully slipped linen strips under my body. I was still lying on the raised cross-pieces that had allowed them to put salt under me, so they could do this with relative ease. They wrapped one layer of linen spirally around my torso. And then they lifted me up and placed me lying on two stone blocks at their knee level—the blocks supported me at the knees and shoulders. When I was higher, with more empty space underneath, it was easier for them to wrap me.

One embalmer took a cup of melted resin in his hands and brushed it on the linen while more resin was being heated on a little fire. After this, they wrapped me up some more, and repeated the whole thing. They slipped the amulets the priest gave them in between the layers. The observing mummies gave a yell every time the embalmers managed to thieve an amulet without the priest noticing—they would put small, smooth pebbles under the linen strips so that it looked like the amulets were still there.

I was surprised at how many of them were stolen this way. And all the embalmers seemed to be in on it! Still, a considerable number of amulets ended up where they were supposed to be. The excitement of the mummies increased every moment, yet there were already some rather disappointed looks—some of them had not thought I could possibly lose so many of my amulets.

All the while, the lector priest kept reading spells from a scroll, declaring what each amulet was supposed to do for me in the afterlife. Many of the spells were carved on the amulets themselves, most of which were on my head and chest. I was wrapped up in spells more than linen, it seemed.

There was the headrest amulet, and more Eyes of Horus and *wadjet* cobra amulets to give protection. The *djed* pillars of lapis lazuli, a most expensive stone, were the symbols of the god of the afterlife, Osiris, and looked like a vertebral column, giving strength and stability. The *wadj*, or green papyrus stalk ensured rebirth in the afterlife, the red *tyet* amulet, and the knot of the goddess Isis were to protect me. Then there were lots of little scarabs, *ankh* amulets galore to represent new life, *shen* symbols for eternity, *nefer* amulets for all things good and beautiful, and many others.

But the most important amulet was the heart scarab, placed over my heart. It was a big scarab that could replace my physical heart, should it be lost, so that I could still go through the weighing of the heart—to see if I had been a good person, my heart would be weighed against *Ma'at*, the Feather of Truth. If it was heavier, I would not make it to the afterlife.

What's that you say? That surely it was heavier than a feather? Well, I made it, didn't I? I wouldn't be telling you about my mummification here if I hadn't. Gravity isn't quite the same thing in the afterlife, so it is possible for a heart to be lighter than a feather here, thankfully! Just to be on the safe side, a spell was

carved on the underside of the large scarab, telling my heart not to talk nonsense about me but to confirm that I had been a good person, worthy of a pleasant afterlife.

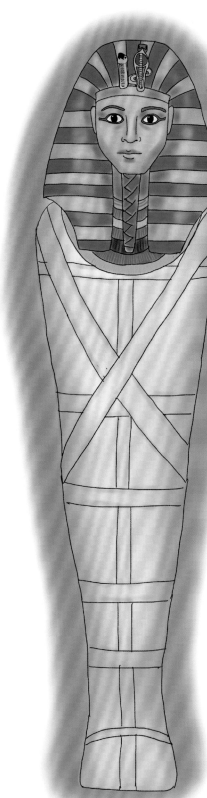

Once my torso was well wrapped, they continued to wrap me into one big bundle, with my hands bent across my chest, holding the crook and flail (the crook being the king's scepter in the form of a shepherd's crook, while the flail was another symbol of royal power—you would never be taken seriously as a king in the afterlife without the crook and flail!). All of this disappeared under the bandages. A beautiful golden mask covered my head and chest, quite like the one you probably already know—the mask of Tutankhamun (my descendant, by the way).

Then they placed cartonnage bandages over me. These were made of linen and papyrus that was plastered (a bit like your cardboard). Some more spells were painted on the bandages. And then a large, broad shroud was placed over and around me, and this was tied in place with horizontal and vertical bandages. I looked like an insect cocoon when they'd finished.

My son let out an amused snort once I was ready.

"What's so funny?" I wanted to know.

"You'll have one heck of a job getting yourself out of there. . . ."

"What?" I was shocked. "But I'm not there, I'm here!"

"Just you wait until the Opening of the Mouth ceremony. . . ."

I did not like the sound of that, not one bit.

"Oh, don't look like that," he said. "Of course I'll come and help you, and so will others as well. All of this is necessary so that you gain your body back. Or would you prefer to fly with the winds to the ends of the earth for all eternity?"

"Erm, no."

"Well, that's that then—you'll just have to endure. And let's hope they didn't use too much resin and oil while wrapping you."

"Why?"

"Too much of them can eat away your flesh and turn you into powder. But whatever the case, you'll be a lot more dark-skinned than before. Resin does that to your skin."

Well, I didn't mind the darker shade of skin, but I did not like the thought of being dissolved into a mere skeleton.

The mummies tallied up the stolen amulets, and winnings were paid to those who had earned them. The mummies disappeared one by one.

"So, what now?" I asked.

"Now we wait for your coffin to arrive. And while we wait, we can watch what they do to your intestines."

10 Canopic Jars and Coffins

They did the same to my internal organs as to my body: wrapped them in linen so that they were neat bundles. These they placed in alabaster jars. Each jar had a different head-shaped lid—these were the four sons of the falcon god, Horus.

The liver went into a jar with the head of a man: Imseti. The lung jar had the head of a baboon: Hapi. The stomach jar had the head of a dog: Duamutef. And the intestines were protected by the head of a hawk: Qebehsenuef.

The jars were placed in a calcite chest specifically made for them.

My names were beautifully carved on the canopic chest in cartouches (meaning my names were inside oval bands that symbolized eternity) and painted in blue. The term 'canopic jar' is a later invention, by the way—we called them *qebu en wet*, 'jars of embalming').

The chest containing all the jars was placed in a gorgeous gilded wooden shrine, mounted on a sledge. Beautiful slender goddesses protected the corners of the shrine, their fingers reaching out to touch the goddesses next to them—Isis, Nephthys, Neith, and Selqet.

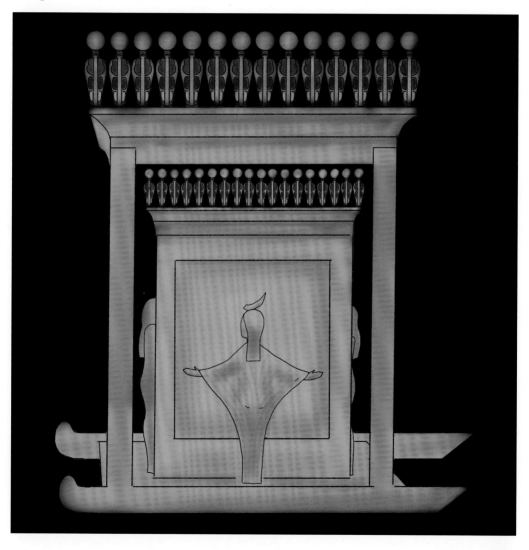

"I am quite pleased with the jars, you know," I told my son, observing the beautiful handiwork.

"Well, you'd better take them with you to the afterlife. If thieves find the chest, they'll throw your intestines away and keep the jars and chest. There's a market for beautiful embalming jars, after all. A little chiseling, and your cartouches are gone, and a new name can be written on the jars. And if you don't have your jars, things might get tricky. It's hard to eat without your stomach! And you want to breathe, drink, and be merry, don't you?"

I decided that the canopic chest would be the first thing I would take from my tomb. A king has to eat and drink, after all, and it had been my favorite pastime during my last decade on earth. I began to ponder what kind of food I would be served in the afterlife, and how it would taste.

And then we waited for the coffins to arrive. Yes, there were several of them! After all, I was the king, and would never manage with only one.

The coming of the coffins took days.

"They do take their sweet time. . . ," I said after a few days, drumming my mummy with my fingers, impatient to get on with it. I was beginning to feel annoyed at being tied to my son all the time, and wanted to have the ability to move on my own again. Also, listening to the neverending reciting of spells by the lector priest was becoming extremely tiresome. I seriously suspected that whoever had written the spells had been off his rocker—most of it made no sense to me at all.

"Let's go and see where they are. . . . They should be here soon." My son yanked me out of the embalming house like one of your modern balloons, leaving behind the lector priest and the guards protecting my mummy.

As we hurried toward my former palace, I saw two large sleds on their way toward the

western Valley of the Kings from the direction of my Mansion of Millions of Years, which was the temple dedicated to my divine cult. (After all, if I had declared myself to be a god, I had to have a temple dedicated to myself.) Huge oxen were pulling the sleds, and indeed they were loaded with my coffins.

They were a glorious sight to see. They shone in the sunlight—they were made of pure gold. They were covered with linen sheets, but it was a windy day and the wind lifted the sheets enough for the gold to show. Every time this happened, a loud sigh rose from the spectators.

Not only priests but also soldiers escorted the coffins, for obvious reasons, though I doubted any thieves could have lifted them one inch, and the oxen were not exactly racehorses, so leading them elsewhere in an effort to steal the treasure would have been a fool's errand.

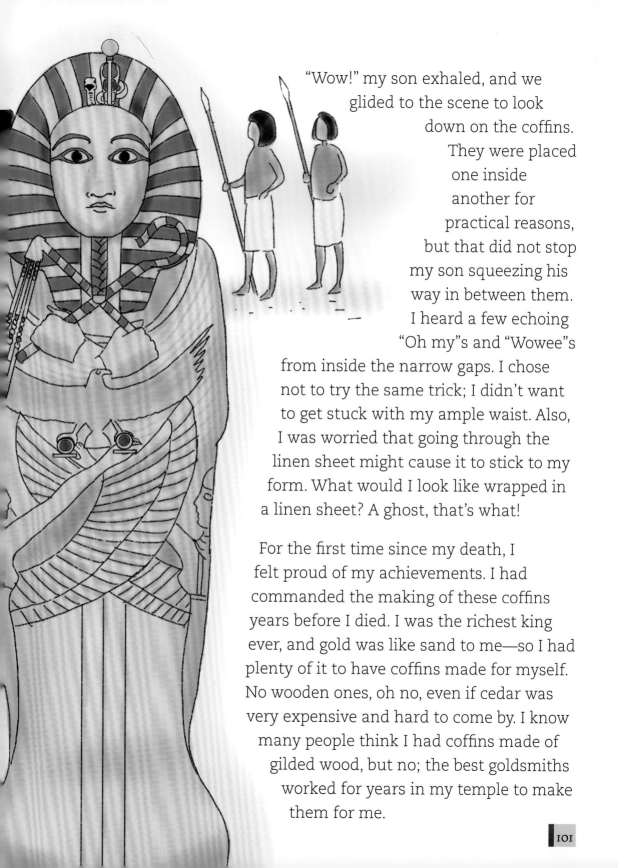

"Wow!" my son exhaled, and we glided to the scene to look down on the coffins. They were placed one inside another for practical reasons, but that did not stop my son squeezing his way in between them. I heard a few echoing "Oh my"s and "Wowee"s from inside the narrow gaps. I chose not to try the same trick; I didn't want to get stuck with my ample waist. Also, I was worried that going through the linen sheet might cause it to stick to my form. What would I look like wrapped in a linen sheet? A ghost, that's what!

For the first time since my death, I felt proud of my achievements. I had commanded the making of these coffins years before I died. I was the richest king ever, and gold was like sand to me—so I had plenty of it to have coffins made for myself. No wooden ones, oh no, even if cedar was very expensive and hard to come by. I know many people think I had coffins made of gilded wood, but no; the best goldsmiths worked for years in my temple to make them for me.

The second sled had all the lids of the coffins, also made of gold, and decorated with jewels and glass inlays.

I was especially proud of the coffin with wings that wrapped around me. Each feather was made of different colored glass or precious stone.

You could have bought any foreign kingdom with just one of these coffins. And I had been so rich that they were only a fraction of my property. I did own the whole land and everything in it, after all, and Nubian gold poured like a neverending stream to my court.

Pulling the sleds was a slow business, much slower than when my body had been transferred for mummification. Again, they were helped along by pouring milk before the oxen so that the ground was more solid, and not just dust.

When the tired animals finally made it to the valley, they didn't stop at the embalming house, but passed it by.

"What? Where are they going?" For a brief moment, I wondered if they were about to steal my coffins after all, but they would surely not have headed toward the closed valley. . . .

"To your tomb, of course," my son explained. "Much easier to put your mummy into the coffins and close the lids when they are already in place inside your sarcophagus. Now your heir needs to perform the Opening of the Mouth so that you get your body back, and so that he may inherit your crown. And your mummy needs to stand up for that occasion. It would be rather difficult to lift the golden coffins to an upright position with you in them, don't you think? They're so heavy that they might just tip over, leaving you lying on your face in the dirt. It has been known to happen, you know. Surely you don't want to bite the dust, too?"

I could see the wisdom of his words. I would not want the last memory of myself to be of a king face down on the ground.

"If you had chosen a wooden coffin, you could be put there immediately, but gold is too heavy."

"Well, I prefer gold nevertheless," I said. "Fitting for a king like me, being divine and all that. When does the Opening of the Mouth ceremony start?"

I think my son made a strange snorting sound when I mentioned being divine, but when I turned to look at him, his face revealed nothing (how could it, with all the wrappings?).

"Well, usually it would start just about now, as your mummy is ready, but it will take time before they get to it," my son explained. "They need to carry all the necessary stuff into your tomb first. Only after that can they lay you down to rest. It would not be proper to bury you first and then spend a week carrying your things into the tomb, disturbing your peace."

"Can we go and see the tomb?" I asked.

"Sure, why not? The others must be there already."

No need for me to ask who the 'others' were. The already familiar bunch of mummies were busy sizing up my coffins. The general opinion seemed to favor the gold and splendor.

My son had to use his elbows to make way for us, which made a hole on the side of one mummy ("Sorry!"), one hand falling off an especially old-looking fellow with dirty yellow wrappings ("Here, let me put it back for you!") and one loose foot being kicked around ("Who's lost his foot? One extra foot here! Oh, there you are. . . . Would you please pass this to the mummy in the corner? Thank you!").

Once everyone knew their place, we observed how the coffins were slowly pulled inside the tomb and toward the actual burial chamber.

It was hard work: first they had to slow down the slide of the heavy coffins at the very steep entrance corridor stairs. Then they had to negotiate the coffins over a deep pit using planks (I had taken *some*

precautions against thieves after all). Then they had to turn at a right angle to the left to reach yet another steep, sloping corridor (stairs here, too). At the bottom of that, they had to make another ninety-degree turn to the right to reach the burial chamber. Then they had to get through a pillared room to the stairs at the end of it. And there, finally, waited my sarcophagus. It was red granite—a novel innovation I was quite proud of. Usually, kings had their sarcophagi made of quartzite, but I had wanted a more splendid final resting place of beautiful hard red stone, red being the color of the sun and of life. Yes, I was very pleased with myself at having chosen red granite.

It took a very long time for the priests and workers to get the coffins to the sarcophagus, and the men didn't look very happy with the job. Wisely, they had placed ropes round each individual coffin and could lift them using these.

The mummies were in great throngs around the coffins to see better, and once in a while one of the living shivered and cast a fearful look over his shoulder, as if sensing their presence. I was sure if they had seen the mummies, they would have run off and never returned. We tend to have quite an effect on the living, for some reason.

"Well, this will take a while," my son said as we observed the sweating men slowly inching the heavy golden coffins closer to the sarcophagus. Even a snail would have outrun them. "You will have years to look closer at your coffins if you want to. Let's get out of here.

Again I was pulled by the linen strip, up the corridors and stairs, and into the world of the living.

"I hope they begin the Opening of the Mouth ceremony soon. . . ." I mumbled.

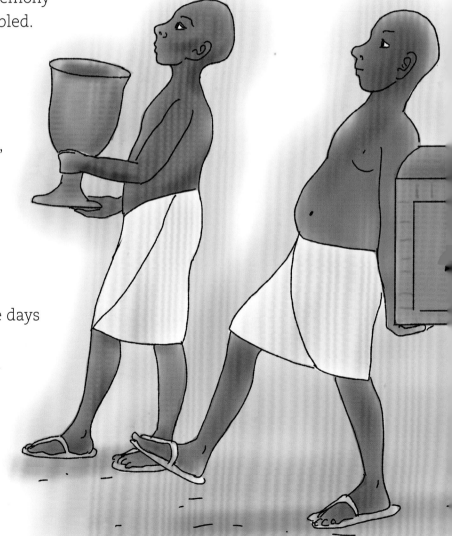

"Nah, not until the coffins are in place, and the treasures have been brought in." Thus my son crushed my hopes of being my own man soon.

After a few more days of being led on a leash by my son, the coffins were obviously in place, because more oxen began their slow journey toward my tomb from the direction of my palace and temple (conveniently situated next to each other).

This time, they brought chests, statues, fabrics, perfumes, jewelry—all the riches you can imagine. They were guarded by so many soldiers that you could barely see what they were guarding, which was good, because the people standing by the roadside looked like they wouldn't mind hiding a golden thing or two in their sleeves—my loyal subjects, who had adored me when I lived!

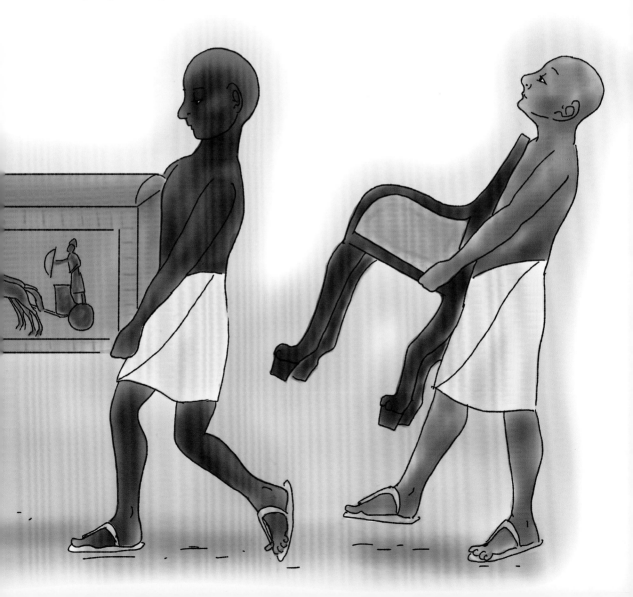

"They're counting the loot." My son echoed my thoughts. "You can bet they're already making plans on how to get their hands on those riches!"

"But my tomb will be guarded!" I protested. "They wouldn't dare!"

"Yes, they would. And the guards will eventually be bribed, I've already told you. It's the way things are. It's up to you to save as many of your riches as you can. The rest will be stolen, make no mistake about that."

The caravan of treasures traveled from my palace to my tomb, where the priests took the valuables and carried them in. Ordinary people were not allowed into the valley at all, and the soldiers made sure that no one approached the tomb. The closest that people were allowed to come was the village of Pa-Demi (also later called Set Maa, or the Place of Truth), where the tomb-builders lived (you may know it by its modern name, Deir el-Medina).

"Want to go in?" my son asked.

"No, I'm sure there are plenty of mummies there already. . . ."

"You got that one right. They're making an inventory of anything you could steal and bring to the afterlife. You will be one popular king here, I tell you. But I advise you not to go into business with anyone before you've spent a few years here. They would cheat you out of your fortune in no time. Better to stay near me—I'll teach you. Of course, should it happen that Mom dies soon, your treasures will be totally safe!"

I had to agree with that—I wanted to see the mummy who would dare cheat my missus. (She has died since the days I'm talking about, and trust me: she is a formidable person in the Duat, or afterworld, and no one wants to anger her.)

"But now I think we should go back to your mummy," my son said. "The moment is near!"

11 Dead and Buried

I was pretty nervous now that I knew my burial was imminent.

"Just stay near your mummy," my son advised, "and remember, we'll come and help you out of your coffins once they've sealed the tomb."

I had never liked closed spaces, and the thought of being stuck inside several coffins deep inside a sarcophagus. . . .

"I don't like this!" I complained.

"Relax. No one has ever remained stuck in their tomb." My son waved a dismissive hand. "At least, not that I have heard of. If no one comes to fetch you, you'll figure out eventually how to get out of there. I've heard a few interesting quarrels when the deceased wasn't exactly liked by their already dead relatives and they sort of forgot to come and pick up the newcomer. The term 'curse of the mummy' actually comes from all those deliberately forgotten mummies who swear and curse in their tomb while trying to get out of their coffins on their own."

I could only hope that I had not been such a bad father that my son would conveniently forget about me. . . . But then again, he had already promised to come and help me.

"Here they come now!" My son pointed toward the mouth of the valley.

And so they did. A long procession approached the tomb. First came the offering bearers—so many of them that I wondered if there would be room in my tomb for all the goods they were carrying.

I heard loud wailing as we glided through the air to meet the procession. I was quite impressed at the number of professional mourners the missus had ordered to show their grief around my coffin.

They stopped in front of the embalming house, and my mummified remains were lifted by the priests onto yet another sled pulled by a pair of fat oxen. The animals had clearly been fattened at a temple: their coats were so shiny, and they were so round. Again, milk was poured in front of the sled.

As soon as I had been placed on the sled, the mourners started their work with great enthusiasm, and wailed and threw dust and ash over their heads, as was proper. I was touched by their eagerness to mourn me.

We followed the procession to the tomb, my son and I. My missus and my heir were sitting in a sedan chair, right behind the sled. I noticed the high priest whom I had last seen shivering with fear under his blankets. I was happy to see that he was walking rather than being carried in a sedan chair, and that he eyed my mummy with definite nervousness.

My missus was calm and poised, and a mere look from her made my heir pull back his shoulders. He was dressed in a leopard skin, a white kilt, and gilded sandals. On his head, he had a broad gold band. I was pleased; this was the first time he had actually tried to look royal. He stole a nervous, sidelong glance at a beautiful young lady walking in the retinue behind the sedan chair. I recognized her—we had chosen her to be his Great Royal Wife. Later, she would be called the most beautiful woman in history (which was not far from the truth).

When the procession finally reached the tomb entrance, the priests carefully lifted my mummy off the sled. They placed it in a standing position in the middle of a mound of clean sand which someone had desposited by the tomb doorway.

A beautiful golden mask covered my head. I looked wonderfully young in the mask, with almond-shaped eyes and a slight smile at the corners of my mouth. My eyebrows and eyeliner were made of real lapis lazuli, and in my *nemes* head-dress stripes of gold and blue glass alternated (I was proud of all that blue glass, as glass was a new invention, made at my royal workshop).

A divine plaited beard, also inlaid with blue glass and curved at the tip, descended downward to my chest, over the broad collar that covered my shoulders. Lapis lazuli and glass glistened together with the gold of the mask. I looked mighty handsome, I will admit that. Mighty handsome indeed.

The *muu* dancers appeared. They performed a sacred dance that was to help my journey to the afterlife. They wore tall openwork reed head-dresses (which looked rather funny, to be frank). They took high steps in the air, holding their thumbs and index fingers straight, and the rest

of the fingers in a tight fist. The steps symbolized stepping over the boundary between the physical world and the afterlife.

Lots of spell-reading ensued. I waited, standing by myself, as advised. And finally it was my heir's turn. He approached my mummy, holding a *pesesh-kef* knife. It was a very sharp flint knife, broadened to a fork at the tip. It was like the knife the midwives used to cut a newborn's umbilical cord, allowing the child to live on its own in the world of the living. Now it was meant to make it possible for me to use my senses in the afterlife. The knife symbolized my rebirth as a mummy.

I was proud of my heir, because he did not ask for advice from the priests. All those years of studying religious scrolls had finally paid off! He recited the spells and prayers in their proper order, and touched my nose, mouth, ears, and chest with the knife. This he repeated four times.

The first time he did it, I suddenly realized that I could stand on the ground again. My son untied the linen strip that had held me attached to his mummy, and the wind did not take me.

The second time, I began to move toward the mummy, like someone was pulling me. The third time, I was sucked right inside it, and suddenly I could feel my body around me again. And the fourth time he repeated the spell, I could see, hear, and smell in my mummified body.

It was the oddest sensation! I could feel all the bandages around me. I could sense the weight of the golden mask. I could see right through it. But, being so tightly wrapped into a bundle, I could not move.

I saw people gathering together, pulling out blankets and baskets of food. They sat down on the valley floor in front of me, and started having a picnic. I saw all the delicacies they had brought with them, and they placed many bowls in front of me, too. Obviously that was not very nice, as I couldn't eat them, but I appreciated the gesture.

Once they had eaten, the priests took me up and carried me inside my tomb. They were chanting spells all the way down to the burial chamber. All I could do was observe the ceiling above me. Only my missus and my heir followed the priests and myself to the tomb.

The room was just as crowded as before; I could see them from the corners of my eyes. The mummies were eyeing my valuables, and enjoying the show.

"Hang in there!" one of them shouted. "Won't be long now!"

"Yes, we'll help you out!" another commented from the general direction of one of my jewelry boxes. "Can I have these turquoise earplugs as a thank you?" A dry hand appeared in my field of vision, showing the plugs in question.

"I could use the perfume bottles for my wife. . . ." A very thin mummy floated above my coffin. "Would you swap them for a pet monkey? My wife doesn't like monkeys—she says I'm quite enough on my own! But she does like perfume, and might let me go out for a beer with my friends if I gave her a nice gift. . . ."

My son appeared next to me.

"Shut up, you!" he snapped at the mummies. "Show some respect for my father's burial!" he shouted, making me proud of him.

The mummies mumbled something, but managed to stand still in what might be called respectful rows (using a little imagination).

I was lifted inside the innermost coffin inside the sarcophagus.
My missus approached, and placed a garland of flowers
on my chest. Then, at her mark, strong men lowered
the golden lid over me. Then two more lids.
And then, finally, there was a loud thump
as the stone lid was dropped into place.

So there I was. Dead and buried.
I listened to the silence for a
while. Then I remembered
that I could see through
the golden mask on my
face. I figured that the
coffin lids would not be
any more difficult to see
through—and true enough,
it was like opening a set of
eyelids, one after the other.

I had ordered a pair of eyes
to be carved on the lid of
my sarcophagus. Usually,
these were placed on the side
of it, because mummies were
laid to rest on their left side
and could therefore see out of
the coffin through the painted
(or carved) eyes on the side. But,
as I may have mentioned, I was a
big man, and putting me on my back
was so much easier. And that is how I lay there.

I had a faint recollection that it had actually been my vizier who had suggested that it would be best to have the eyes on the lid. A wise man, I had to admit. He was related to the man who ran the temple workshop that made stone statues and sarcophagi. The last time I had seen them talking, the stonemaster relative had clearly been telling a story of a fish that got away—he was standing with his arms open wide, shaking his head. When they saw me, he and the vizier blushed for some reason and hurried off, complaining about unfinished business. Only later the thought came to me that the big thing they were talking about was not a fish but me.

Because I was lying on my back, I had a clear view of one of the mummies, who was now sitting on my sarcophagus, trying to stuff a necklace of mine into his wrappings.

"Hey!" I yelled from inside the coffins. "That's mine!"

Much to my surprise, he seemed to hear me, and with an apologetic grin slid down to the floor.

"Give me that. . . ." I heard my son say. "Now, everybody come and help—we need to lift the lids!"

It took an extremely long time. As my son had informed me, things were even heavier for the mummies and ghosts than they were for living people. But they had clearly done this many times before. I could observe them from inside my coffins, and saw that the mummies were in such a tight pack that the ones on the outskirts were literally standing on the wall, their bodies horizontal, pushing the nearest mummies with all their strength. These in turn did the same to the mummies in front of them, all the way to the ones with their hands on the side of the lid, and finally the strength of dozens of mummies was enough. They pushed the stone lid to one side, and slowly it gave way and fell to the floor, breaking into two pieces with a loud boom and crack.

This was followed by quieter creaks and groans as the mummies gathered whatever bits and pieces had fallen off them during their struggle.

All the golden coffin lids had silver handles, and the mummies rummaged through my grave goods to find the linen chest. They took rolls of linen, and put these through the handles. The mummies divided into two groups on each side of the sarcophagus,

and, using the linen, lifted the coffin lids off me one by one and pushed these to the floor as well.

Then I was finally lifted out of the inermost coffin. With experienced hands, they took the golden mask off my head and started unwrapping me. Rolls and rolls of linen fell to the floor, until finally all that was left was the innermost layer of wrappings. This meant that my arms and legs were finally free! I carefully tried to move them and they obeyed. A big sigh of relief! I then took off enough wrappings from around my head that I could open my eyes again.

At this, all the mummies cheered.
If I had been alive, I am sure a tear or two might have moistened my eyes, but all that salting had effectively drained me of any moisture in my body.

Now the mummies no longer looked like ghosts to me. They appeared totally solid. Just to be sure, I patted my son's back, and a cloud of dust rose into the air. I could see it because the oil lamps the priests had left in the tomb were still burning.

"Well, well. . . . Thank you, everyone," I said to them.

"Now, show us what you want to take with you to the afterworld," my son said. "And start with all those amulets. They are very valuable in the betting business."

The unwrapping had caused all my amulets to fall on the floor. I gathered them in a little basket. With the help of my son, I then piled up the valuables I wanted to take with me on the floor. The scribe who had been taking the wagers at my mummification made a detailed list of these.

"No one is to steal anything," he said with authority. "So the ones who have things hidden in their wrappings will now put them on this pile!"

No one admitted to anything, but a few pectorals, rings, and small statues flew through the air, and landed on the pile of treasures on the floor.

Someone opened the false door of my tomb. A false door to you who are alive, but very real for us that are dead, as it allows us to enter the Duat.

And so we stepped through the false door, carrying everything we could possibly carry. I personally carried my canopic chest, to be sure I would have my stomach, heart, liver, and lungs in the afterlife.

"We shall have time to come back and gather more things," my son said. "But you'd better take as much as you can now. You never know how quickly the looters will come—might be years, might be days."

"But we expect to be compensated for the help we gave you," said the thin mummy who had asked me about the perfume bottle.

I was so happy to be back in my body, heading for my new life in the Duat, that I promised him that bottle. He grinned so widely that if he'd had any teeth left, I would surely have seen them all. I had made my first dead friend, it seemed.

And that is the story of how I became a mummy and entered the Duat.

As for what happened next, well, that is quite another story. . . .